Master Critical Thinking

Learn To Think Intelligently, Improve Problem-Solving Skills, Make Better Analysis, and Upgrade Your Life

Henrik Rodgers

Table of Contents

Introduction

I remember the first time I had enough money to buy a car. Like most other teenagers, after high school, the best car I could afford was a used one. Still, that didn't stop me from dreaming big and wanting the most automobile that I can get for every dollar that I had to spend.

Me and my brother would go through the used car listings of many classified sites that featured cars for sale in my area. After several days of going through several selections and narrowing it all down, I had my eyes on two remaining contenders. Everything else was either too expensive or there was obviously something wrong with them.

One model came from a line of fairly decent racing cars. This brand has often been associated with racing and sports cars. The other model was a sportier version of a fairly decent car line.

My brother was more practical than me. He told me that I should pay close attention to the maintenance history as well as overall wear and tear of whichever car I buy. With his help, I was able to check out both cars.

The first car, in hindsight, looked a little bit beat up. Its best years obviously were behind it. But still, I just fell in love with the fact that if I spent my hard-earned dollars with this unit, I would actually own this very famous brand.

The other car was in better shape. It also had its maintenance records in order. Everything checked out. When we looked under the hood, it seemed that it was well maintained.

What do you think happened next? That's right. Being a teenager, I went with my heart. I went with the sporty reputation behind the brand of the first car.

In other words, I was not looking at facts. I let my emotions get the better of me.

It's not like I stopped thinking. I knew what was going on. But in my head, the fact that I got to own this very special and historic automotive brand meant more than other more objective considerations.

Fast forward six months and, you guessed it, I found myself at our local corner store mechanics garage. My car had to go to the repair shop because of wear and tear issues.

Well, I let that slide. But soon enough, after about three months, I found myself back at the mechanic shop. And this time, I was facing $3,000 in transmission repairs.

When I asked the mechanic if there was a chance that my car's other systems would experience trouble, he said there may be a good chance because the car, it turns out, was really badly maintained.

At that point, I started to think critically. I wasn't thinking critically before, but the choice before me now was pretty stark.

I spent a total of $6,000 on the car. It's going to cost $3,000 for the transmission, and there is a high probability that it's going to cost thousands of dollars more should other parts of the car go south.

At this point, I basically decided to cut my losses and trade in the car for a brand-new unit.

Now, don't get excited. The brand-new car was definitely less sexy and definitely did not have the kind of automotive engineering pedigree of my trade-in. Still, this was a very hard lesson learned.

I was ready, willing and eager to trade in my youthful dreams of driving around in a car that had a very prestigious logo in exchange for something more trustworthy and dependable.

My experience taught me that a little bit of critical thinking can definitely go a long way.

Critical thinking involves being able to look at facts and come to hard conclusions. Often times, these conclusions don't line up with what we would like or what we would expect. Often times, they come with quite a bit of a negative or ambivalent emotion. Still, critical thinking is crucial because they help us make better informed decisions.

Critical Thinking and the Power of Facts

A lot of people are under the impression that when you are forming an opinion or analyzing a set of stimuli, that you are automatically thinking. The problem is, for the most part, you are just operating out of preexisting opinions.

In other words, you already started with the conclusion and you're just trying to plug in facts that would support the conclusion that you already had. This is the mirror opposite of critical thinking.

Critical thinking requires a certain level of personal maturity because you cannot step up to the facts with a preexisting explanation or conclusion that unites or makes sense of the facts. In other words, you let the facts lead you to the conclusion instead of you coming in with some sort of preset idea or agenda.

This is what gets a lot of people in trouble because the whole idea of maturity is that you only need to see certain patterns and you can safely jump to conclusions. While that may apply in many areas of life, it doesn't apply across the board. And in the areas that it doesn't apply, it can lead to a tremendous amount of trouble.

In this book, I'm going to teach you the basics of critical thinking and how you can overcome your natural tendency to use your biases, prejudices and preconceptions to lead you to the conclusion that you think you already know.

The scary thing about critical thinking is that it requires you to step outside of your ego. It really does. It requires you to let go of your comfort zone on both intellectual and emotional bases.

This is not always easy. If your pride and ego are tied into your ability to make snap decisions or you are a particularly lazy thinker, this is going to be quite difficult.

Now, of course, in many areas of life, critical thinking may not be all that welcome or even necessary. For example, if a friend of yours was coming to you because she just broke up with her boyfriend of ten years, she may actually just need a shoulder to cry on and a sounding board.

Nine times out of ten, people in that type of situation are not really looking to solve their problem. They're just looking for another person to physically be there and give them emotional support. They're looking for somebody to just listen to them as they try to sort through their issues.

They're not exactly looking for you to slice and dice and logically analyze their issues. In fact, in many cases, relationships are often strained when the person looking for comfort feels that he or she is being put on the spot or even judged.

With that said, there are many other areas of life where a little bit of critical thinking can definitely go a long way. If you want to make better decisions, if you want to be a more effective leader, if you

Let's get one thing clear, all of us are human beings. All of us are capable of making bad decisions. Nobody has a monopoly on this. But the problem is, if you have really poor critical thinking skills, the chances of you making a bad decision are quite high.

Now, everybody's entitled to making a bad call from time to time. In fact, it happens to the very best of us. The problem is, you know that you have to make a change when it seems like regardless of what you do, you seem to make a bad call almost each and every time.

Something has to give. It's only a matter of time until a really big disaster occurs because of your bad moves.

You Build Failed Systems

People who do not think critically are more likely to create bad systems. Systems involve processes that work with each other toward a common outcome or output.

For example, business people put up business establishments. But if you analyze the jobs of the people there and the tasks that they do, they can actually be categorized into systems that feed into each other. There are sales, marketing, accounting, product sourcing, supply chain management, and so on and so forth.

If you are a very sloppy thinker, chances are, the systems that you build either don't fit together or are not optimized for the best results. Whatever the case may be, you may be putting yourself and your finances in a bad position.

At best, you are settling for cents on the dollar. At worst, you're actually laying the foundation for a major financial disaster in the future. In fact, if you have particularly weak critical thinking skills, you're going to experience bankruptcy sooner rather than later.

You Give Bad Advice

If you're not a very critical thinker, it's very likely that the advice that you give is not optimal. That's a polite way of saying that people should not be listening to your advice.

Because, usually, people are looking for great outcomes. Most people would rather get an efficient piece of advice where they risk very little and get back a lot. In other words, they'd rather get the most output for as little input as possible.

Unfortunately, if you are a bad critical thinker or a sloppy thinker, your advice would be very inefficient, assuming it produces any outcome at all.

It Leads to Stronger Prejudices

Let's get one thing clear. Everybody has prejudices. Everybody has biases. Nobody's really free from this.

The problem with bad critical thinking or sloppy thinking is that these tend to make your biases worse. You develop mental habits that would reinforce your worst biases instead of disrupting them.

You have to understand that the more prejudiced and biased you are, the more you put yourself in a competitive disadvantage.

We live in a market economy and market players who are free from irrational prejudices and biases are more likely to spot and take advantage of opportunities that present themselves in that market.

They have a higher likelihood of taking advantage of systemic efficiencies because they are not held back by biases or prejudices that may have been formed from incomplete information or flat out lies.

If you are a sloppy thinker, you are more likely to let your emotions or your deference to tradition or group-think override your natural ability to detect patterns and spot opportunities.

The Bottom Line

Sloppy thinking leads to massive disadvantages in life. It erodes the quality of your relationships, it puts you at a competitive disadvantage, and it also makes bad decisions worse.

The sooner you can improve your critical thinking skills, the sooner your life will improve across the board. It may not jump out at you, but eventually, you will be laying the foundations for better results later on.

Chapter 1: The Definition of Critical Thinking

The US National Council for Excellence and Critical Thinking uses this definition for critical thinking: "the intellectually disciplined process of actively and skillfully conceptualizing, applying, analyzing, synthesizing or evaluating information gathered from or generated by observation, experience, reflection, reasoning or communication."

People use such information to guide their beliefs about a situation or a body of ideas. They then take action based on this belief.

Critical Thinking and Judgment

A more streamlined definition of critical thinking is the objective analysis and evaluation of an issue in order to form a judgment.

Both definitions above proceed from the same place. Both place an equal importance on the primacy of being objective.

Objective thinking, of course, involves looking at the evidence and facts and using reason or generally acknowledged reasoning to come to a conclusion.

It's Important to Pay Attention to What's Missing

When defining critical thinking, it's important to zero in on what's missing. What do you think is missing in both of the definitions above? The obvious answer, of course, is emotion, tradition, or prior habitual patterns.

Interestingly enough, according to a recent study, consumers make decisions in an impulsive way. They don't look at what they're about to do and break it down in terms of the outcomes that they're looking for. They don't check out the facts a certain way and plug this into some sort of mental formula to come up with an informed choice.

It would be great if consumers operated this way, but let's be honest here. If people were objective and critical thinkers, there probably would be less products sold on this planet.

I know that that's quite a bold claim to make, but let's get real. A lot of the products that are sold currently in the marketplace are products of hype and exaggeration. In fact, when you look at the wide range of product options available, there's a lot of space for substitution or retention.

Take the case of the Apple iPhone. The current iPhone models cost north of a thousand dollars. Well, if you are a critical thinker and you look at what it does objectively and what your needs are, there's a high chance that you can come up with a well-reasoned decision to hang on to what you've got.

Maybe your iPhone model is several years behind, but when you look at what you actually need and your actual usage patterns in the space of a week, it may well turn out that your "old model" does plenty. It fits you like a glove.

Just using critical thinking in this scenario, it wouldn't make sense for you to blow $1,000 or more on a new model.

Fortunately, or unfortunately, this is not how most consumers think. Instead, consumers think impulsively. They buy impulsively.

What the research indicates is that when people make the actual decision, they do so impulsively.

Maybe they do so on an emotional basis, or maybe they got triggered by sales material.

For whatever reason, they make the plunge. But when asked to explain their decision, they come up with all sorts of reasonable-sounding explanations.

The researchers who studied this phenomenon frame it in terms of "buy impulsively and explain logically." You'd be surprised as to how logical many of these explanations may seem.

But it turns out that when you look at the objective condition and financial realities of the people making these choices, critical thinkers would say that it wouldn't objectively make sense for them to make the decisions they made.

Breaking Down Critical Thinking

To make this book as practical as possible, let's break down the different elements of critical thinking.

I wouldn't want you to proceed with a very convoluted, highly compact definition because it's not going to serve you all that well. You want something that is practical. You want something that you can slice and dice and apply to a wide range of situations on a practical, day to day basis.

With this in mind, here is practical thinking, broken down into several abilities.

Critical thinking is the ability to think:

- In a reflective way
- Independently
- Logically
- Based on evidence
- After sensible evaluation of facts and evidence
- In context with other pieces of evidence
- Using logical connections methodically without emotional input

In some, critical thinking is all about the ability to think objectively, logically and clearly. It enables you to think beyond your biases and prejudices and evaluate facts directly.

When you come up with a decision, it is only after you have filtered all these facts through clear reasoning.

What Critical Thinking is NOT

This probably not the first time you have picked up a book on critical thinking. After all, the phrase "critical thinking" is a fairly common phrase. People talk about it quite a bit.

Unfortunately, just like most other concepts that are quite popular in our culture, its meaning tends to get confused. It's very easy for the concept of critical thinking to get mashed into or confused with other concepts and practices that are not critical thinking.

In this short list, I'm going to share with you what critical thinking is not.

Critical thinking is not:

- The pure analysis of data
- Being correct or wrong
- Winning an argument
- Criticizing another person's position
- Becoming aware of deep emotional truths and personal revelations

It's important to flesh this distinction out because there are so many misconceptions about critical thinking. If you're unclear as to what it isn't, it's very easy to walk away with all sorts of faulty ideas as to what it is.

Unfortunately, what makes this all difficult is the popularity of certain misconceptions about critical thinking. I need you to be aware of some of these misconceptions so you can get out from under them in your efforts to build up your critical thinking skills.

The first misconception is that critical thinking only has one overarching definition. As you can tell with the definition that I gave you, it falls under different situational definitions because it all depends on what you're thinking about and in what context.

Another misconception is that this type of skill can only be taught in certain academic disciplines or technical fields where there is explicit problem solving to be done.

According to this thinking, certain academic training gives you the proper methodologies with which to think critically.

This is not true. Somebody who works at a fish market can be a great critical thinker because they have to make important decisions.

Likewise, somebody who farms for a living has to also be a critical thinker because his or her choice regarding farm inputs can and do play a major role in whether the farm would make a good profit, a decent profit, or suffer a loss.

Another common misconception about critical thinking is that it is completely based on somebody's perspective.

On its face, this misconception is flat out wrong. After all, critical thinking involves objective facts and reasoning.

That's how you know you're thinking critically – when you're viewing facts on an objective basis and applying your reasoning skills on them. This means that the conclusion that you arrive at will be the same as somebody else who chose to be objective when looking at the same set of facts.

The problem is, a perspective-based approach merely sounds realistic. It is actually quite deceptive because it posits or actually argues the opposite – that critical thinking is purely subjective.

If your ability to think critically is based primarily on your personal perspective and experience, then everything would be subjective. There would be no such thing as critical thinking because different people looking at the same set of objective facts will walk away with completely different reads on the situation.

Critical thinkers can agree to some conclusions, and then disagree as to what they mean. Still, they agreed on certain conclusions based on objective facts. This has little to do with your perspective – although your opinion regarding the impact, consequences or long-term effects of what you have concluded can be based on your opinion.

By the same token, we can take the objectivity of critical thinking to extremes. No one can really say that critical thinking will always lead to perfectly "objective" results. We should also pay attention to context.

If anything, critical thinkers should focus more on how objective their process is and, to a certain extent, their conclusion. But as far as conclusions go, there has to be some leeway for context.

Another misconception about critical thinking is that kids don't have any critical thinking skills. This is not true. When properly trained and encouraged, kids can develop adequate critical thinking skills.

Finally, there's this idea that only certain types of people are capable of critical thinking. This is a very dangerous idea because you're edging very close to the conclusion that some people are born critical thinkers and most others aren't. That's not true.

Critical thinking, just like self-discipline, patience and other important and invaluable human traits, are learned behaviors. They are products of the way we live out our lives. They are not foregone conclusions. They don't drop in our laps. We don't stumble upon them through the lottery of birth.

If you want to be a more critical thinker so you can make better decisions, you can choose to learn to be that way. You don't have to resign yourself to the fact that you simply weren't born a critical thinker.

Now, with all these misconceptions and definitions out of the way, we're going to jump into the often-contentious topic of why many people have a tough time with critical thinking.

disrupt their existing frame of reference. They think that this is more of a bother than it is worth.

Well, the long standing idea of "opposites attract" is actually not scientifically valid. If you look at the actual research and evidence, it isn't true. But this idea continues to persist, and we can all thank sloppy and lazy thinking for this.

A Lot of People are Mentally Uncomfortable with Critical Thinking

To take things to the next level, a lot of people develop a laziness when it comes to critical thinking because, at some level or another, they feel discomfort.

I know it sounds kind of extreme to position this as some sort of "pain," but yes, there is such a thing as mental pain.

You have to understand that if you are trying to figure out something new or you're trying to look at a situation with a fresh set of eyes, it can be quite painful because the "pain" emanates or comes from your ego cracking.

You have to set aside your ego. You have to overcome your pride. You have to push back or roll back on your personal programming to look at situations from a fresh set of eyes and objectively come up with a new conclusion.

Most people don't want to go through this because the slow, painstaking effort of overcoming biases seems so inefficient. It seems like it's not worth the bother compared to just jumping to a conclusion with both feet. You know that there's a high chance you're going to be wrong, but since you've seen this before and there's a tremendous amount of emotional comfort and convenience involved, you do it anyway.

You Have to Overcome the Reasons Above If You Want to Become a Better Critical Thinker

Please understand that regardless of whether you work in academia or not, or whether you work with any kind of analytical subjects or projects, you need critical thinking to be a more effective human being.

The reason why there are so many problems in the world and the reason why there are so many relationships that are not functioning to their fullest potential is because people are too eager to jump to conclusions. People are too eager to think at shallow levels and in sloppy ways. This leads to a less than optimal quality of relationships, decisions and life outcomes.

If you think you tend to make the wrong decisions or if you think that there's quite a bit of anxiety or regret in your life, or you're frustrated at some level or another, you might want to become a more critical thinker.

You might not need to go see a shrink. You might not need the help of antidepressants or antianxiety medication. It may well turn out that a lot of your personal frustrations is because of the fact that you don't practice critical thinking at optimal levels.

This book is going to teach you how to become a better critical thinker using 7 techniques. I'm going to give you a quick overview in Chapter 3. And in Chapter 4, we're going to jump into these techniques at a step by step basis. See you in Chapter 3.

Chapter 3: How to Be a Critical Thinker Using These 7 Techniques

This chapter is an overview of the 7 techniques that will help you become a more critical thinker. Each technique has steps that you can follow. Some of them also have clinical studies that support the validity of each technique.

Please understand that the material below is intended to serve as a framework. Everybody's different. We all come from different walks of life. We definitely have different sets of experiences.

These differences, as small as they may be in many situations, do add up. This is why it's really important to keep in mind that there is no such thing as some sort of magic bullet solution to sloppy thinking.

If you want to improve your critical thinking skills, use this framework and fine tune them based on your personal experience. By taking full personal ownership of these techniques and tweaking them or modifying them to fit your daily experience, you maximize their value.

You also increase the likelihood of incorporating these techniques into your daily activities. Eventually, they become automatic. How come? They have become part of you.

Here are the 7 techniques for improved critical thinking skills, in no particular order. While I suggest that you try them all out, it's completely up to you as to which technique you start with. Regardless, you have to use all of them because they do have a scaling effect.

- Keep an open mind
- Develop and nurture your intellectual curiosity
- Learn to spot and resist any appeals to emotion
- Refuse to look at things at face value
- Make sure to always stop and reflect when presented with things to think about
- Identify and overcome your negative self-talk or negative thoughts
- Be aware of your current listening skills and constantly seek to improve them

Chapter 4: Always Keep an Open Mind

To become a critical thinker, you have to look at the information presented to you as if your mind is a blank slate or a "blank enough" slate.

This is important because when you come into any situation with a preexisting conclusion in desperate need of supporting facts, you're not really doing yourself any favors. What you're doing is you're basically just cherry picking the information presented to you.

And whatever decision you come up with is not optimal. How can it? It's not based on the actual facts you have in front of you, but based on nonexistent facts or based only partially on what exists or is completely a product of your imagination.

Whatever the case may be, you're trying to push a square peg in a round hole. Not only is it frustrating, but it actually doesn't help you become a more effective person.

Instead of obsessing about how you wish things were, focus on how things really are. And the first step to all of this, of course, is to look at objective facts and let them lead you to a conclusion.

This is impossible if you don't have an open mind. When you have a closed mind, you really have a template in your mind that you're just trying to fit all facts and experiences through.

Being Open Minded Enables You to Consider All Possible Answers

When you're truly "open minded," your initial attitude is that you are looking for as many different answers as you can find. You understand that while these answers are not going to be all equally valid or valuable, you're looking for as many different options as possible so you can rank them later on.

The idea is, the more options you have available to you, the higher the chance you will actually go with the very best one. Compare this attitude with the idea that there is already one universal answer, and if you can't find it, you're going to patch it together based on the information you have in front of you.

Which one is more realistic? Which one deals with the facts on the ground? Which one leads to better consequences? The answer should be obvious.

Additionally, being open minded enables you to accept a conclusion that might be different from what you normally expect. This is a big deal because the more you do this, the more you break free of your biases.

Biases are confirmed when you keep seeing the same outcome or you keep accepting the same outcome. Your initial conclusions get strengthened because you keep picking a certain outcome. What if that outcome was not warranted or justified by the facts on hand?

Being Open Minded: Easier Said Than Done

As awesome as the discussion above may be, let's get real. Most of us have a tough time being open minded. After all, we are born with certain expectations. We come from certain backgrounds that give us certain biases and prejudices.

Nobody's really free of this. Nobody's immune to this. Worse yet, not only do we have this set of beliefs that we inherited from our parents or our social group, we tend to be surrounded by people who share the same beliefs.

We also tend to associate with such people. By doing so, we tend to reinforce these beliefs. This happens without us being conscious of it. We don't even have to try. This is our personal context.

Unless you're aware of this, it's very easy for this to undermine your efforts at being open minded.

The Essence of Being Open Minded

To be a truly open-minded person means you have to assert your independence. That's really the bottom line.

People who have a tough time being open minded and are basically just held captive to their own biases and prejudices are people who really have a weak sense of self.

They consult with people who already believe the same way they do. They know this, that's why they run to those people for instant validation. They know what the answer is. They're not really expecting some sort of surprise.

Independent thinkers and open-minded people have these traits because they have a clear sense of self. They know where they begin, and they know the boundaries of their personal self.

They also have a clear idea regarding personal intellectual boundaries. They know the difference between liking and admiring people who have a certain set of beliefs, yet respecting themselves enough to stand by their own distinctive beliefs.

This is a big deal because if you have parents who have a certain viewpoint, just because you have a different point of view or opinion, it doesn't mean you love them any less. It takes maturity to get this.

Other people would feel betrayed. Other people would feel that they're letting their parents or their social group down if they actually assert their right to independent thinking and they exercise their critical thinking skills.

The Bottom Line

Being open minded enables you to learn, grow and strengthen your independent sense of self as well as boosting self-confidence.

What is the Impact of Being Open Minded When It Comes to Critical Thinking?

In a study released in 2015 in the Journal of Translational Medicine and Epidemiology, study participants were tasked to complete a transdisciplinary orientation survey that had 12 questions.

They were asked whether they disagreed completely, agreed somewhat, or agreed completely with a wide range of questions. This is called a spectrum agreement or disagreement survey.

They were asked questions like, "I generally approach scientific problems from a multilevel perspective that encompasses both micro and macro level factors" and "My research to date reflects my openness to diverse disciplinary perspectives when analyzing particular problems."

There was a total of around 76 randomly picked professors from a wide range of disciplines.

It turned out that the study participants who were more open minded in terms of the disciplines that they source information from produced work that were independently rated higher by third party analysts.

Put simply, people who are more open to other academic disciplines and perspectives tend to produce research that is of higher quality.

By being open minded, you don't just focus on what you already know or your field's methodology. You look at other fields and you explore other methodologies. This can lead to better work quality.

Similarly, when it comes to political views, a Yale University study, published in the journal "Advances in Political Psychology," notes a correlation between scientific curiosity and political open mindedness.

The research consisted of two studies. One was experimental, the other was observational.

First, the researchers surveyed 2,500 people with a wide range of questions that were presented as part of some sort of marketing survey. Questions regarding people's attitudes towards science were mixed in with questions regarding popular entertainment, politics, finance, sports, and other issues.

By mixing up the questions this way, the survey respondents didn't know that the researchers were actually trying to gauge how interested in science they were.

Using this observational study, the researchers found that people who are interested in science tended to also have a high interest regarding scientific issues that had significant societal risks like nuclear waste disposal, fracking, and climate change, among other highly politicized issues.

In the experimental portion of the study, the researchers split up 3,000 people into two groups. Each group was asked to choose between two varying news stories about climate change.

One headline was written in a way that it would give a "climate realist" orientation. The other headline was positioned towards a more "skeptical" view of climate change. These headlines were also written in a way that could either support a person's existing belief about climate change, or surprise them.

Among the people who were curious about science, they preferred to engage with headlines that surprised them, even though these may run counter to their existing political views about the topic.

This study highlights the fact that people who are open minded about politics tend to also be more curious about science.

Being open minded necessarily means that you expose yourself to challenging and potentially opposing ideas. This requires the willingness to expose oneself to new ideas.

It also highlights the fact that you really cannot claim to be open minded if you are not willing to expose yourself to information that runs counter to what you think you believe about a certain issue.

Step by Step Guide to Being Open Minded

Step #1: Read as many different sources as possible about the topic you're interested in

When you do this, you're embracing the unknown. You're not looking for any set conclusion. You're not looking for any "established" or "prequalified" source. Instead, you're just allowing yourself to be exposed to a wide range of information.

Also, to be more open minded, learn how to stop saying "no" to new experiences and new ideas. Instead, make "I'd like to try" your default answer. You'll be surprised as to how quickly your perspective can be challenged, enhanced, or flat out changed by your willingness to just be exposed to new information.

Step #2: Examine any situation from multiple angles by default

Our default approach to any kind of new experience is to obviously look at it from our existing perspective and our own personal angle.

Try to flip the script. When you think of any political issue or social issue, you read up on different commentators with different world views.

For example, if you are thinking about fracking, look at what conservatives say, and look at what libertarians say, and also look at what liberals and leftists have to say. This way, you can look at the different perspectives they bring to the table and the facts that they use to support their position.

By looking at the broad spectrum, you can see not only the conclusions that they've arrived at, but more importantly, the facts that they use to arrive at that conclusion. This gives you a better view of the issue and exposes you to a wide range of perspectives that might disrupt, surprise, or even change your mind.

Step #3: Educate yourself outside your comfort zone

I know this sounds like a tall order, but it isn't. In fact, if you just pick up a new hobby, you are already doing this. What's important is you allow yourself to be personally open to new experiences.

You don't have to stick to an iron-clad routine. Just because you've done things a certain way since forever, it doesn't mean that you are doomed to repeat that pattern until you're dead.

You can mix things up by learning a new language, doing things that you're not particularly good at and try to improve your skills that way, traveling more extensively or more often, and simply reading more.

When you do this, you change your expectations. And, more importantly, you change your default response to new experiences.

Chapter 5: Cultivate Your Personal Intellectual Curiosity

One of the most powerful ways you can become a critical thinker is to simply allow yourself to be more curious. Please take note of the phrase "more curious." All of us, at a certain level or another, are already curious. This is part of the human condition.

If you like to gossip about your neighbor, or your friends from school, or somebody in your circle of friends and acquaintances, you're being curious. If you like to think about what other people are thinking, you are, at some level or other, being curious. Curiosity is hardwired into the human condition with varying degrees of intensity.

The question is not choosing to be curious or not. The biggest challenge you have, as far as becoming a more critical thinker goes, is to choose to become more curious. This is actually one of the most practical steps in becoming a better critical thinker.

You can start with what you are already doing. You don't have to do something completely new. You don't have to go out of your way. You don't have to adopt a new routine. Just focus on the things that you already do in the span of a typical day.

The secret, if you want to call it that, is to look at different ways of looking at the things that you're already interested in, or think of newer ways of doing the things you are already engaged in. This encourages you to become more intellectually curious. Instead of thinking habitually, you start looking at your daily routine with a fresh set of eyes.

You go from some sort of "automatic thinking," that there's only one way to do what you normally do, to looking at things from a structural perspective. For example, if you if you go from point A to point B every day, maybe you should try another route. It may well turn out that another route is more efficient. You may discover new sites. It may be a more enjoyable route.

Similarly, if you do certain tasks at work, don't automatically assume that the way you've been doing things is the most efficient, most effective, and most productive. You don't know how much more productive you could be unless you try new things.

Discover the power of asking why

A lot of the explorations that I discussed above can be triggered by enhancing your intellectual curiosity. The good news is you don't have to bend over backwards. You don't have to do anything out of the ordinary. It turns out that by simply asking why, you jog not only your creative faculties, but you also trigger memories.

Why is this a big deal? Well, whatever it is you are working on, or think you have mastered, there was a time when you didn't actually know what you think you know. You were groping around; you were feeling your way around, and you were trying to figure things out. This early stage of learning might have exposed you to different ways of looking at whatever it is that you do and think about habitually now.

Asking "why" triggers you to think about alternatives. Now, you and I know that these alternatives may not be the most efficient; a lot of them might lead to dead ends. But don't let that discourage you. The fact that you ask "why" will help you unpack what it is you're doing, and how you go about doing things.

When you ask the question "why," you get to the essence of why you do the things you do. This enables you to peel back many different layers of explanations that you have given yourself throughout the years. It may well turn out that you chose the way you do things not for less than optimal reasons. You may discover that there may be a better way to do what you normally do.

Constantly asking "why" enables you to be curious about alternatives. This is the firm foundation of critical thinking. You cut straight to the chase. When you analyze what it is you're doing and how you go about doing things, you are focusing on an issue in a fairly superficial way.

If you really want to get to the heart of the matter, you need to break everything apart by dropping the question "why" on it. It acts like a bomb that blows a part the structure of what it is you're trying to understand. You are then left to rely on your curiosity and critical thinking skills, to piece things back together.

When you think about why certain things exist, you unpack all the processes that led you to doing things a certain way. This can open your mind to alternative paths. These may not be optimal, but at least they shine the light on either a better way, or more likely, how to optimize what you are already doing.

The proper role of curiosity

Curiosity motivates you. It involves critical thinking, but it's more valuable in terms of the motivation it gives you. When you are curious, you are motivated to look at things in terms of first principles. You are less likely to assume that the way you're doing things and the way you are thinking about things are the most optimal. You get that preconception out of the way, and this opens your mind to viewing your situation in a different enough way where you can achieve some sort of breakthrough.

This is normally hard to do, believe me. People get intellectually lazy. If you are like most people, you're probably thinking that you have too many other things to think about. There are so many other worries on your plate. But when you allow yourself to be curious, you get the motivation you need to look for new ideas and to examine old patterns, so they could possibly lead you to new places. Even if they don't, It's still a good idea to exercise curiosity, because it can pay off with other tasks or other issues in your life.

Indeed, in a study published in 2011, in the Journal Perspectives on Psychological Science, researchers conducted a meta-analysis of around 200 studies involving 50,000 students. Based on this massive data analysis, the researchers found that there is a strong correlation between intellectual curiosity and future academic excellence. They found that curiosity is a pretty good predictor of how well somebody would do in the future as far as their academic performance goes.

In fact, among all the different factors analyzed by the study's researchers, curiosity ranked next to conscientiousness as a solid indicator of future academic excellence. In another study, published by researchers with the University of California Davis in the journal Neuron in 2014, when the brain activity is analyzed during peak periods of curiosity, MRI scans showed up predictive patterns that match the same scan patterns of the brains of subjects who were ready to learn something new.

The researchers conclude that when people are curious, they are more likely to learn. In other words, if you are an open-minded curious person, this can lead to more rewarding learning experiences since social experiences tend to involve learning about other people. Then curiosity makes positive social outcomes more likely.

Finally, in an April 2013 study, published in the Journal of Personality, researchers report that there is a positive correlation between curiosity and a wide range of important psychological adaptive behaviors. This includes having a non-critical attitude, the ability to think outside the box, the tendency to look at any problem with a playful attitude, a healthy sense of humor, positive emotions, and a healthy tolerance for a certain level of uncertainty and anxiety.

The researchers show that a little bit of curiosity in unstructured social interactions can lead to a higher level of adaptive behaviors, which can enable people to get along better with others. Social interactions, after all, can be quite stressful. Apparently, researchers have found that the more curious people become, the less likely they are to adopt a non-critical attitude as well as being less likely to be defensive. They are also more likely to be playful and unconventional in their thinking. They are also more likely to be humorous.

Step-by-step guide to cultivating a sense of curiosity; here are just some basic tips on how you can develop your own personal intellectual curiosity.

Step #1

You need you need to have an open mind

Be prepared to learn from sources that you may not be all that comfortable with or familiar. Just assume that you can learn something from anybody at any time.

Step #2
Don't think anything for granted

Just because you've seen something before, or you've heard people say something before, doesn't mean that you can automatically just process that information the same way you did yesterday or the day before. Don't take things for granted. Look at them as something new.

Look at them as saying something or responding to something in a new way. Although you know that this is not exactly new, because you have seen this before, but assume that it is, and allow yourself to be curious that way.

Step #3
Ask open-ended questions that trigger your personal curiosity

Instead of simply saying statements to people or asking questions that you know the answers to, ask open-ended questions. Ask questions that can lead to different conclusions or different answers. If you're stumped, asked the handy question "why."

Of course, you don't want to overdo this. You don't want to annoy people, because that would defeat the purpose. Still, ask questions that trigger your curiosity. Ask yourself these questions as well.

Step #4
Don't be in a rush to label things

Don't think that just because you have seen something, that it is predictable, boring, or conventional, don't be in a rush to judge. Just allow things to play out while entertaining your sense of curiosity.

Step #5
Assume that learning is fun

If there's anything that you can assume, assume that learning something new is fun. It isn't threatening, it isn't a waste of time, it isn't reinventing the wheel. Just assume that it is fun. You'd be surprised as to where this attitude could lead you.

Step #6
Allow yourself to read all kinds of reading material

It is very easy for people to pigeonhole themselves. It is very easy for people to say, "Well, I'm into political websites. I love political opinions and commentary, and business online newspapers." Well, it's time to expand your mind by reading things you don't normally read.

Sure, you may have all sorts of preconceptions about a certain type of online content, like gossip sites, or celebrity sites, and personal interest websites. But allow your sense of curiosity to just scan these, and at least widen your scope of interest. The good news is if you have allowed yourself to be a little bit more curious, you'll find something to be curious about.

Chapter 6: Be On The Lookout For Any Appeals To Emotion And Resist Them

This is a good time to review Aristotle's famed list of logical fallacies. I know that this technique focuses primarily on appeals to emotion, but people make all sorts of logical fallacies. They appeal to authority, they appeal to emotion, they commit no true Scotsman logical error, they employ strawman arguments, etc.

The best place to start, of course, is to be aware of appeals to emotion. After all, this takes many different forms. Usually, when people start an argument with a riveting personal story, you know that they're eventually going to appeal to emotion. This is one of the most common forms of illogical thinking.

This is why I suggest that you start with this type of logical fallacy, but don't stop there. While this is the most obvious and easiest to deal, allow yourself to be curious about the full range of logical fallacies that people can employ.

Why resist appeals to emotion?

When somebody tells a tearjerker story, they're not really appealing to your ability to work with facts. They're not engaging your ability to use logic on facts and evidence to arrive at a conclusion. Instead, they are want to trigger you so you can either sympathize with them, or get so upset that you really can't argue your point.

However way they choose to do it, they're manipulating you. An appeal to emotion is simply a manipulative way to try or make a point without dealing with facts or logic. The worst part to all of this is most of the time, it is intentional. Most to the time, people who appeal to emotions know that on a purely logical and objective basis, they don't have a case.

Seriously, they don't have an argument, they know that coming in. So what do they do? They intentionally trigger you so you become irrationally sympathetic to them, or they upset you and anger you so you can't think straight. Either way, they win. Don't let them win.

If you are in an argument, keep it to the rearm of facts and let it stay there. Alternatively, if you are in a sort of collaborative group and this person is trying to appeal to people's emotions to manipulate the group, stand up for everybody else by calling out the person in a respectful way, or redirecting the conversation to where it needs to go. Nobody's really being served if the sort of group solution you come up with is based on emotion and other nonsense instead of facts and reasoning.

Several studies show that emotion-based "reasoning" can be very problematic. For example, in a University College London, a brain imaging study, published in the journal Science, showed that the way a question is posed can be interpreted differently by respondents, depending on their emotional states.

In this study, 20 women and men went through three 17-minute brain scans while getting suggestions to gamble. They all had a starting pot of English pounds valued at $95. When the participants were told that they can keep 40% of their money if they didn't gamble, the participants went on to gamble only 43% of the time.

Now when wording was changed to losing money, an interesting thing happened. When they were told that they can lose 60% of the money if they did not gamble, 62% of the time, they gamble. Interestingly enough, the odds of winning were actually explained in detail to each participant beforehand.

Obviously, the chances of winning were the same. But the way the question was framed had a significant impact in skewing their decisions.

The brain scan images showed that the amygdala, which is a nerve center in the brain that is linked with strong negative emotions like fear, was very active during each gambling decision. When they were told that they would lose 60% of their money, their amygdala was fired up. On the other hand, when the question was framed in terms of keeping the money, other areas of the brain, linked to positive emotions like empathy, were more active.

This shows that our emotional state has a significant effect in our brain's decision-making process. In fact, you can make the argument that the emotions overrule reasoning, given the fact that the odds of winning and losing among the participants remained the same. The only difference was the framing of the question regarding their gambling decision.

Similarly, in a June 2014 study, published in the journal Frontiers in Psychology, out of the Justus Liebig University in Germany, 30 participants were tested one by one regarding their emotional state. After their emotional state was determined, the participants then were asked to take a popular IQ test.

These were broken down into three IQ tests. In total, there were 13 items in three categories. The categories were matrix tasks, calculation, and sentence completion. The groups were then broken down three, with each group being assigned different sets of questions in descending order of difficulty.

Once they have finished the test, the participants were then given different verbal feedback designed to manipulate their emotional state. People who tested initially for negative emotions, and were assigned the difficult questions, were told, "We are sorry to say that the analysis of your data showed that your performance was below the average student performance."

The neutral group was given the feedback, "The analysis of the data showed that your performance was on par average student performance." Finally, the group of people who had positive emotions were told that they performed above average.

After all groups were given these statements, they were asked to take the emotion test again. And after that, they were asked to take another intelligent selection test. The study found that when people are operating under a negative emotional state, they perform less successfully in tasks. These are people who, regardless of their reasoning abilities, show that emotional content can disrupt rational faculties and performance.

Follow these tips to help you better manage your emotions to improve your critical thinking skills

Tip #1
Avoid instant reactions

The moment you get emotionally triggered, take a step back and refuse to react. Instead, take a deep breath, take some time out, walk around a little bit, and then try to process the information. You'd be surprised as to how much better you will be able to handle what would otherwise be a slippery slope of bad decisions.

Tip #2
If you're emotionally upset, find a default healthy outlet

If you find yourself emotionally triggered or upset in any way, come up with a default answer. What is the that the default action you would take when you know that you are in a negative emotional state? Some people listen to music, others literally take a hike, they step out and walk around. Other people go to sleep, take a nap.

Whatever the case may be, there has to be a healthy outlet for what would otherwise be a very negative emotional state. If you feel that you are about to get emotionally worked up, go to the gym and get a workout going. Take out your frustrations there.

Tip #3
Step back to the big picture

Life is filled with all sorts of twists and turns, we don't always get what we want, we don't always get our way. That's just the way life goes. The good news is, just because you experience a setback now, doesn't mean that you've lost it all. Look at the big picture, maybe things aren't working out, or there are issues at this point, but look at the big scheme of things.

You would be able to see that the ultimate goal or outcome is worth the hassle. This gives you the motivation to try to calm down and figure things out at this stage, so you can eventually get to where you want to go. Nobody's really being helped by you running around like a chicken with its head cut off.

Tip #4

Identify your personal "happy place"

All of us have a personal happy place. I'm not talking about a specific geographic space where you can reliably feel good about yourself and everything else happening in the universe; not all of us have that luxury. Instead, I'm talking about a memory. Do you remember the time when you felt accepted, complete, understood and loved? Do remember spending some time at a place where you felt completely at peace, and you are fully comfortable in your skin?

The good news is, regardless of how turbulent your life is, you can at least come up with one that one memory in time. Identify it, focus on it, and memorize its details. When you find yourself in a stressful situation, think of that mental happy place. Remember, there has to be a mental state where you feel that you don't have to be somebody else, you're not trying to prove something, you feel completely at peace, there is harmony in your mind, and you feel calm.

To maximize the effect of your personal "happy place", practice mindfulness. The more you train your mind to zero in on the present moment, the stronger that sense of inner calm becomes.

Tip #5
Learn to forgive yourself

Granted, not all of us have a happy childhood. A lot of us went through abuse of one form or another. Maybe your mom used to yell at you a lot. Maybe your dad physically abused you. Maybe you were bullied as a kid. Whatever your past trauma is, please understand that it doesn't have to define you. You don't have to carry it around for the rest of your life.

The worst part about those traumatic experiences, is the more you think about them, the more you pick at the scabs of those emotional wounds. What do you think happens when you pick on a scab? That's right, your skin bleeds again. The wound never really heals. The worst part of all of this, is as you get older, you will read into your memories of past trauma, your current insecurities.

Maybe you got sexually abused as a child. Well, you can look at those abuse episodes and read into them the abuse your husband puts you through today. You layer on emotional abuse, you blowup emotional abuse component of the sexual abuse, and you just end up making things worse on yourself.

Stop it. I know this is easier said than done, but you'd be surprised if you find yourself in a situation where the memory starts the flesh in your mind and you just say to yourself, "I don't have time for this, it's happened in the past, I cannot change the past. All I have is now, and I'm not doing myself any favors if I let the trauma of the past poison my present."

Admittedly, this is hard. It definitely takes a tremendous amount of effort, but the good news is, if you are able to overcome this, you'll be able to make better decisions because your negative emotions will not warp the decision-making process. You owe this to yourself.

Tip #6
Don't be afraid to ask for help

If you're struggling with emotional issues (maybe you're too sensitive, maybe you're harboring emotional trauma from the past, or you just have bad emotional coping skills), get help. Now, this doesn't necessarily mean that you have to go see a psychiatrist or psychologist, although that is always a good option. You can talk to a friend.

Talk to somebody who knows how to keep your confidence. Talk to somebody you can trust.

Alternatively, you can assume an alias and post on bulletin boards where people sound off. You can post your experiences on a blog. You can even write a book. Believe me, one of the most cathartic things you can do is to write a book.

I was helping a friend of mine put together his memoir about his father. He didn't end up publishing the book, but he ended up with something far more valuable than book royalties. In the process of me helping edit, and put together, and organize his memoirs, he was able to forgive his father.

His father wasn't really a very encouraging person. Everything that my friend did in life, and all the decisions he made were simply not "good enough" for his father. For the longest time, he rejected his father's advice. If his father said, "turn left", you can bet that my friend will turn right.

It took him a while to achieve stability in life. But when his father died, he had all these notes from well-wishers and he asked me to organize a memoir for his father. He just finished giving a eulogy, and when he looked through the organized memoir, which is basically just a chapter by chapter treatment of the memoir, my friend still had to write out the "meat" of each section.

He broke down and cried. He realized that as much as he hated certain aspects of his dad, he loved his father so much. In fact, a lot of his hate for his father was really just thinly veiled pleas for acceptance from his father. He was so proud that he couldn't bring himself to ask a very basic question to his dad, "Why can't you accept me for who I am? Why can't you accept me because I'm not you?"

What got to him was the fact that it turns out his father also struggled with the same issues with his grandfather. His grandfather was a multimillionaire. His father didn't graduate college, hitched a ride across the United States and Europe, and basically blew through his inheritance. It turns out that the reason why he blew through his father's inheritances is that he did not want any of his father's money.

If he were to keep that money, it would remind him that he would always be standing in the shadow of his father. My friend's father carried this with him throughout his life and it poisoned his relationships. It was only during this period, where we were compiling his father's memoirs, that my friend saw this and discovered this very hidden part of his father's history. That is when he broke down and he realized that he loved his father more intensely than he was aware of. That's when it became real.

Do yourself a big favor. If you are struggling with any kind of personal issue that puts you in a negative, or a very touchy, emotional state, write it down, just write it out. Write what's on top of your head, there's no need to edit yourself. Later on, try to organize it in a time line. You will notice that there are certain gaps. Fill in those gaps, dig through your memories.

Here's a tip that I gave my friend that enabled him to achieve that emotional breakthrough with his father's memoir: do not judge what you write. It is very easy for us to filter the stuff that we choose to remember, don't do that. Just dump it out. You'd be surprised as to how much of your personal trauma you can get over by simply getting it down in writing, and reading it several times. Eventually, you will see the big picture, and before you know it, you will be able to move on.

Chapter 7: Always Go Beneath the Surface

You know you're practicing critical thinking when you go beyond face value. It's very easy to say that you shouldn't take things at face value. It really is. In fact, you probably have heard this before.

The problem is no matter how often you hear this piece of advice, it's very hard to do. Let's just get real here for a second. Everybody's busy. Time is a luxury.

It is no surprise that most people with rather go with shorthand understanding of reality. How does this work? If you've seen a pattern before and you know that it leads to a certain outcome most of the time, once you see part of that pattern, your mind goes on auto-pilot. You automatically assume that outcome, as closely associated with that pattern, will appear.

This applies to many areas of our life. This enables us to pick service providers like lawyers, doctors, or bankers. This also enables us to navigate otherwise tricky social situations.

It definitely saves a lot of time because you're not doing any thinking. All you're doing is you are assuming certain things based on what you see at face value.

The problem with this approach is obvious. You're not actually doing any thinking. You're doing pattern recognition. You're not much different from how a frog sees the surface of a pod. The color field of a frog's eyes is very different from that of a human eye.

The good news is it doesn't have to be overly complicated because it only needs to see quick changes for it to send signals to the frog's brain and the frog can make an instinctive decision. If it sees something moving on the surface when two seconds ago nothing was moving, depending on the size and the placement of that thing, it may be food for the frog.

Believe it or not, this is how most people think on a practical level. If you were to stop people in their tracks as they make these "automatic" decisions, they probably would talk a good game with you. They would probably say, "Well, I've done my research before or I've done this before and I know what happens next."

The problem is there may be better options. The problem is the decisions may be very inefficient. Unfortunately, they would be the last to know because we as a species usually don't go beyond face value.

This hasn't always been the case when you were younger and you were seeing the world with the fresh set of eyes, you were a bit more curious, but as you got older and as you were able to absorb more of other people's shared experiences, you started thinking more automatically.

This is the reason social media is littered with fake news. People only need to see certain news presented in a way that they agree with or in a way that they expect and that's good enough for them to click the Share button.

It seems like no matter what Facebook chooses to do, people still manage to spread fake news. After all, there's no controlling people's almost automatic tendency to take things at face value.

Indeed, in a March 9, 2018 study published in the journal Science, fake news spreads faster and contaminates wider social networks than verified stories featured on Twitter.

To understand how the fake news phenomena, MIT researcher Soroush Vosoughi did a deep data analysis of records from Twitter. They looked at which tweets were looked into and debunked by different fact-checking websites. Using intensive data analysis software, they were able to filter out artificial traffic created by bots that infest Twitter.

After all was said and done, they were able to isolate 126,000 fake news items that were shared on Twitter. These items were retweeted 4.5 million times by around three million individuals.

The starting conclusion was people are more likely to share fake news on Twitter instead of accurate news. In fact, according to this research study, fake news was 70% more likely to get a retweet than actual verified news.

This is due to the fact that people take things at face value. They assume that something is true because it plugs into certain patterns that they are used to.

How does this happen? A lot of it has to do with online peer pressure. If you've ever been on Reddit, you would know that there is a tremendous amount of pressure put on people to upvote or approve of certain content that they may not wholly agree with.

In fact, they might be ambivalent about it, but they are under pressure to go along to get along.

This is called "crowd-sourced judgment" and this has a very strong effect on the quality of news being shared on social media. People are more likely to just take things at face value because of this added pressure. You don't want people to downvote you. You don't want people to leave nasty comments.

At first, this is obvious but, eventually, you get used to it and you end up behaving online at social platforms in a way where you tend to reinforce groupthink. This goes a long way in popularizing fake news as well as certain opinions that people may not specifically agree with on an individual basis.

Don't underestimate the power of crowds to create some sort of artificial "authority." This was the conclusion of a study published on January 28, 2019 in the Proceedings of the National Academy of Sciences.

Step-by-Step Guide to Going Beyond the Surface

Step #1: Be aware of the information you're looking at

Before you get triggered by the headline, the title, or the tags of the information you're looking at, take a step back. What is this information about? Who is this aimed at? How can you categorize this information?

By looking at the big picture, you can understand what you would normally expect from this information and thereby guard against any kind of automatic thinking on your part about that category.

Step #2: Look for objective indicators of quality

When somebody shares a news item with you or is sharing some gossip, it's very tempting to just bond with that person. It's very tempting to just say, "Well, this is just between you and me" or "I'm just bonding with you by listening to whatever junk you have to share."

The problem is you're not doing the other person any favors nor are you doing yourself any favors by being an uncritical recipient of this information.

Instead, step up and be a responsible participant in the information communication process by looking for objective indicators of quality.

What are these? Is there a definite source? Is this person just saying, "Well, something happened somewhere, I don't know exactly where and I don't know exactly when but this is what happened."

You focus on what happened and it's very emotionally triggering and you forget about those other important details but, believe it or not, space and time and other indicators should play a big role in your determination of whether to believe that piece of information or not.

Step #3: Quickly verify the information

If somebody tells you on social media that somebody died or said something outlandish, a quick check on Google News can get to the heart of the matter. Don't be so quick to click the Share button. Don't be so quick to retweet because you don't want to be late as far as current events go. Don't let social pressure get the better of you. It's much more important to avoid looking like a fool sharing fake information

Step #4: Investigate for yourself

This is a very tough piece of advice because, hey, let's face it, most people don't have the time to do it, but if you want to truly benefit your social network by sharing only quality information with people, put in the effort to actually dig for information.

The worst aspect of fake news is that a lot of these are so well-crafted that they can pass for the truth. You have to look for supporting details or you have to look for consequences and that's how you can undermine the seeming truthfulness of these pieces of information.

Step #5: No need to judge

I know it's very tempting to give people who have misled you a piece of your mind. You have to understand that not everybody is a critical thinker like you.

When you practice all the steps above, you hone your critical thinking skills. The more you do it, the better of a critical thinker you become.

Congratulations. Pat yourself on the back. You're one of the few who have chosen to think critically instead of remaining part of the massive army of sheep out there who are just blindly passing along bunk information.

With that said, knowing that you are a critical thinker is enough. There's no need to beat people over the head to remind them of your intellectual superiority. It may well turn out that they are actually smarter than you on an IQ point per IQ point basis. The only difference is they're lazy thinkers.

Chapter 8: Always Take the Time to Stop and Reflect on Information You're Trying to Process

If you want to make better decisions, you have to avoid the tendency to rush through the decision-making process. A lot of people do this because they feel that they don't have enough time.

Let me tell you, if you rush through a fairly important decision, you are going to have to find time later on. How come? It takes time to reverse the effects of the bad decision you made. Wouldn't it be a better use of your time to take a little more time in the beginning so you can come up with a better decision and avoid all sorts of unnecessary drama?

Another reason people seem to rush through the analysis decision-making process is they feel that they would look dumb to themselves if they agonize over the details. They feel that they are beyond this and that they should operate at a higher level.

If you think this, you are just fooling yourself. It really boils down to skills. Either you have critical thinking skills or you don't.

It's perfectly okay if you don't because this is one of many skills you can choose to learn. It is an acquired skill. It is not something that some people are born with and most people aren't. You can pick it up.

Do yourself a big favor, take the opportunity to stop and take your time when making a decision. A bit of time and space can go a long way in terms of the quality of your choices.

Believe it or not, critical thinking skills on a practical basis are actually more important than IQ scores. Seriously. When it comes to making good decisions in your life, focus less on your intelligence and focus more on the process. That's right. Focus more on becoming a more critical thinker.

In a California State University study in the Thinking Skills and Creativity journal, researchers studied the relationship between IQ and the importance of critical thinking skills as far as real world decisions go.

Participants were tested for their IQ and they then tested people based on real world outcomes as far as their decisions go. They would rate the quality of people's decisions from mild, mildly bad to severe.

For example, if you were fined late fees for returning a video rental, that's a mildly bad decision. On the other hand, if you came down with a sexually transmitted disease, that's a fairly severe decision.

It turns out that people with higher levels of critical thinking, as determined by tests, had fewer severe life decisions. In fact, when correlated with IQ, the chances of you making better decisions are higher if you scored better on critical thinking skills than if you had a high IQ score.

This is due to the fact that a key part of critical thinking is the ability to take a step back and reflect. People with high IQs tend to think in terms of associations and predictions based on patterns. These don't always pan out.

Step-by-Step Guide to Stopping and Reflecting

Step #1: Focus on your goal

It's very important to identify and focus on your goal. What exactly are you trying to achieve? What is the point of the decision you are about to make? Remember, the decision is oftentimes not the goal itself. It's part of something bigger. Be aware of this.

Step #2: Take the time to weigh your options and use this time effectively

It's one thing to say that you should take a step back from taking action; it's another to actually do something about it. Make no mistake, just stopping and reflecting is not enough. You have to be doing something while you have refrained from making a decision.

This is the time to gather information. This is the time to look at the evidence. This is the time to overcome your feelings and look at things the way they are. This is not idle time mentally speaking.

Step #3: Look at what happens next

You have to understand that in the span of any given day, we have a tremendous amount of choices to make. Most of the time, we go through these choices on an automatic basis. We don't even think about the consequences or long-term effects.

When you have a big decision or a mid-sized decision to make, look at the effects it would have. Start with the obvious and then look at possible other affects. This pushes you to be a more critical thinker because you realize that different choices have different ranges of effects. It may well turn out that the way you normally make a choice leads to a less-than-optimal or less-than-efficient outcome.

This is a great revelation so look at the consequences and see if there is a choice that can lead to better outcomes.

Step #4: Clearly explain your choice to yourself

Before you carry out your final decision, ask yourself about your choice. Explain it to yourself. Does it make sense? Can you clearly and cogently explain or summarize your decision?

Let's put it this way, if it doesn't make sense to you, don't expect it to make sense to somebody else. Your choice may lead to negative consequences.

Step #5: Take clear action

Sometimes when people make bad decisions, it's not because they picked the wrong choice. Instead, they made bad decisions because they didn't go all the way through. They hesitated. They didn't go through the whole process. They didn't do the right things at the right time with the right people and, for whatever reason, they didn't produce the right outcome.

If you make a choice and you took the time to reflect and everything checks out, go through with it. Execute it clearly. This is how you ensure that it will work.

Chapter 9: Overcome Your Negative Self-Talk and Negative Thoughts

What do negative self-talk and a negative internal monologue have to do with critical thinking? You have to understand that critical thinking is linked at some level or other with self-confidence. If you are not a critical thinker, chances are you're not really all that confident about your ability to make sense of taking control of every single situation and making it make sense as far as your goals and your outlook are concerned.

A lot of people think that certain things are just the way they are and they just go through the motions. People with low self-confidence tend to do this because they think, at some level or other, it's all a foregone conclusion. Why should they rock the boat? They're not going to make much of an impact anyways. They are afraid that they can't make an impact because they don't have it in them. They don't trust their abilities enough to make much of a difference.

If you want to be a more effective critical thinker, you have to override any kind of negative internal monologue that you run on autopilot in your mind. These may be limiting beliefs that tend to frame your personal reality a certain way.

These rob you of your willingness and sometimes capacity to think critically. Either you are second-guessing yourself all the time or you just simply rob yourself of the motivation to think in a critical manner.

Whatever the case may be, you end up in the same place. You try to get a lot of confidence from automatic thinking or thinking by simply going through the motions.

It is no surprise that people with low self-confidence and low self-esteem tend to make lower quality decisions. They do it themselves. They feel that they're incapable of anything better.

You have to start somewhere and one way to do this is to neutralize all that negative self-talk so you can become more confident and allow yourself to think more critically. These two processes work hand-in-hand because the more confident you become, the more likely you would be to keep trying to think critically and this can improve your decisions.

When you notice that you've been making better decisions, you feel better about yourself. You feel more competent. Your self-esteem increases and this leads to you trusting yourself more and you become even more confident and you think even more critically and this unleashes another wave of positive results.

You can either do things in a way that leads to an upward spiral or you can stay in that negative feedback loop you're in.

In a study in 2013 published in PLOS One journal, researchers studied people who worried a lot and the quality of their decisions. It turns out that improved critical thinking skills can reduce or enhance worrying. In other words, what you bring into critical thinking plays a big role in enhancing that downward spiral or upward spiral I mentioned above.

You either improve by getting into a positive feedback loop or you make things worse for yourself through a negative feedback loop.

Step-by Step Guide to Quieting Negative Self-Talk

Step #1: Be aware of your self-talk

Write down your internal monologue. You can freeze it if you focus hard enough. The key here is to avoid judging yourself. Don't go into this process assuming some sort of answer. Don't expect anything. Just document the thoughts that go through your mind. This is a stream of consciousness exercise.

You should be able to see a pattern. Allow yourself to have a "It is what it is" attitude towards your thoughts. You're not there to change them. You're not there to judge them. You're just documenting everything you become aware of.

Step #2: Practice mindfulness on your internal monologue

There are many mindfulness techniques available. You can research them on the Internet. They're pretty much everywhere. What's important is you are able to freeze your attention on the present moment.

Whether you're using transcendental meditation or some sort of other mantra-based mindfulness or you're simply just counting your breath, focus your attention on the present moment. You will reach a point where you can actually perceive your thoughts. It's as if they are mental movie images.

Don't judge them. Just allow them to form, become very visible and highly defined, and then slowly melt away. It's kind of like watching clouds pass by overhead. It may seem like the clouds are not moving at all because the wind is very weak but, eventually, they will pass by.

Observe your thoughts this way and eventually you will adopt the same attitude. Just as you really can't avoid a cloud passing overhead, you can't avoid your thoughts passing through. No amount of judgment or negative emotions is going to help you.

Instead, just acknowledge that this thought is passing by. Don't judge it. Don't let it trigger some sort of negative memory. Just let it pass.

Step #3: Adopt this general mental attitude

When you become aware of your internal monologue, let it play out. Just let it pass. When you judge it or when you get emotionally triggered, you actually absorb the internal monologue and usually it's negative. It leads to worry, stress, and frustration. Just let it play out. Eventually, once you become accustomed to this mindset, your internal monologue becomes neutral.

Chapter 10: Learn How to Listen Well

Have you ever noticed that with a lot of people, you only need to ask them questions about what they're doing and what they like to do and other things about themselves and they will have a favorable view of you?

This happens to me quite a bit. I talk to a lot of people and I really have to stop myself. I really do because instead of talking about myself or talking about things that I'm interested in, I always turn the conversation to what they're about and what they like to do.

This has many positive benefits. First of all, it shifts the center of attention to that other person. Let's get real here. All of us like the limelight. We like to be the center of attention. We like to be the center of the discussion.

I know we're supposed to be modest. I know we're supposed to be selfless. I mean, that's the ideal, at least, but let's get real here. People like to be the center of attention.

When you consciously do that and you ask open-ended questions so that the person can continue to talk about themselves, what they like to do, on and on, they become comfortable around you. They start to like you. That's a great benefit, right?

Also, when you give people the opportunity to talk on and on about themselves and what they're interested in, you give yourself the opportunity to know enough about that other person and their interests so you can talk about your common interests.

In a way, when you talk to people this way, the conversation you have can be filtered through your experiences and interests but, at the same time, look like it's all about them. It's a win-win situation. They feel comfortable.

In fact, research study after research study shows that likeability often turns on how similar people think they are. Since you're focusing on stuff that you're already interested in as they present these things, they can see your interest; they can see your curiosity; and they are more motivated to talk to you.

This is the essence of listening. It's all about stepping outside of your ego and allowing yourself to be curious about what the other person is interested in. Everybody's got stories to tell.

I can't even begin to tell you how many times I've talked to random strangers who just open up their life story to me. One example quickly comes to mind. I was waiting at a bus station in college on my way back to campus. A lady sat down next to me and it was obvious that she was feeling stressed and worried.

I said "hello" and we exchanged pleasantries. Then I pointed at something that she was wearing. That was enough to get her to talk about her leaving her husband, worrying about the kids, and whole set of other issues.

First of all, I let her talk; and second, I refused to jump in. I didn't ask questions that were judging or leading. Instead, I asked her about how she felt about each thing that she was sharing and what her plans were.

When you let the other person lead the conversation and you just present yourself as a sounding board and as some sort of structuring device for the conversation, the person will share a lot more information. The more information you have, the more you can process and this hones your critical thinking skills. This also takes your communication skills to a whole other level.

As the old saying goes, "We may have one mouth but we have two ears." This means that it's a good idea to listen twice as much as we talk. After all, it's very hard to learn when you are talking and interrupting people.

It's also important to find something, anything about the person's story that you can emotionally relate to; and when they ask you to tell your story, always focus on that emotional connection or commonality and this triggers another round of sharing on the other part of the person. They feel better; you feel better.

It is also one of the most practical ways the practice compassion. All of us are hurt at some level or other. All of us are feeling inadequate or incomplete at some level or other. We all have that in common.

Some of us put on a better show. Some of us actually go to lengths to try to fool other people into thinking that we're perfectly fine. Deep down inside, we know we're not.

Do yourself a big favor. Cultivate your listening skills. In the space of any given day, there are a tremendous amount of opportunities where you can listen to people. Don't talk over them. Don't shut them down. Just let them talk.

In a 2015 study published in the International Journal of Research Studies in Language Learning, one hundred Iranian students were asked to fill out a TOEFL listening comprehension test as well as a critical thinking study. Researchers saw that there was a strong correlation between levels of critical thinking and a person's ability to listen to and comprehend new information.

Tips for Improving Your Listening Skills

Tip #1: Choose to talk less

Let's get one thing clear. It's very hard, if not impossible, to listen and talk at the same time. Let the other person talk. Ask open-ended questions so they can keep talking.

Tip #2: Adopt a listening posture

I'm not talking about your physical posture. I'm talking about your attitude. When you have properly prepared to listen, you're not out to make a point. You're not out to win an argument. You're not out to prove that you're better than the other person.

You're not out to do any of that. Instead, you are there to absorb and understand information.

Tip #3: Project non-verbal signals that make both of you comfortable

People are not going to share information with you if you look like you're judging them. They're less likely to talk at length if it looks like you're in a hurry to go somewhere.

Choose to be present in the conversation. A little eye contact goes a long way. Also, repeat certain things that they are saying so they can know that you're on the same page. This is how you make them feel comfortable around you, and this increases the likelihood that they will continue talking.

Tip #4: Make sure there are very few distractions

When you are listening to somebody, turn off your mobile phone. This is the least you can do. Give them that much respect.

When you do that and when you demonstrate that in front of somebody, you're basically saying to them in no uncertain terms "Who you are and what you're about to say are important enough to me that I am cutting back on the distractions by turning off my mobile device." This is a big deal especially if you are dealing with a very touchy situation or you are involved in an emotionally charged discussion.

Tip #5: Put yourself in the shoes of the speaker

When somebody is telling a story, imagine yourself going through that same situation. Not only does this open an emotional communication between you and the speaker; it also enables you to be properly motivated enough to understand whatever it is that they're saying. This increases your comprehension skills and also enables you to get a big picture view as to think more critically of what they're saying.

Please understand that in this context, critical thinking doesn't mean criticizing the other person or critiquing them. Instead, it's all about communicating more clearly by processing the information well enough so as to foster good conversations.

Tip #6: Don't be afraid of silence

In any conversation, they will be a lag. There will be points where people will try to collect their thoughts. Sometimes, it's as basic as somebody trying to catch their breath. Don't think that just because there's some silence or some lag that the only way to interpret this is that it's awkward. Just let it flow.

Conclusion

Critical thinking is crucial if you want to improve the quality of your decisions. There is no such thing as a decision that requires absolutely no critical thinking. The truth is the quality of your life can improve dramatically if you just learn how to think more critically.

You are less likely to hang out with the wrong people. You are less likely to send off the wrong signals. You are less likely to make bad calls.

You have to understand that human beings are social animals. Critical thinking is crucial for optimal social interaction. If you want people to respond to you in the very best way possible, you better to think critically and let it influence your communication skills.

Similarly, a bit of critical thinking can go a long way in helping you avoid victimization. We live in a rough world. There are lots of people out there who will try to lie, manipulate, and cheat. That's just part of the game.

The good news is a bit of a critical thinking goes a long way in exposing these people. These individuals may have defrauded other people but it doesn't mean that you are necessarily their next victim.

With the proper critical thinking skills, you will be able to see whether a deal is too good to be true or whether you're allowing your emotions like greed and a fear of scarcity get the better of you. Make no mistake, if you want to take your life to a whole other level, critical thinking is crucial.

DISCLAIMER

Adherence to all applicable laws and regulations, including international, federal, state, and local governing professional licensing, business practices, advertising, and all other aspects of doing business in any jurisdiction in the world is the sole responsibility of the purchaser or reader.

38112181R00061

Printed in Poland
by Amazon Fulfillment
Poland Sp. z o.o., Wrocław